HONG KONG

NICOLA BARBER

WORLD ALMANAC® LIBRARY

Please visit our web site at: www.worldalmanaclibrary.com
For a free color catalog describing World Almanac® Library's list of high-quality books
and multimedia programs, call 1-800-848-2928 (USA) or 1-800-387-3178 (Canada).
World Almanac® Library's fax: (414) 332-3567.

Library of Congress Cataloging-in-Publication Data

Barber, Nicola.
   Hong Kong / by Nicola Barber.
     p. cm. — (Great cities of the world)
   Includes bibliographical references and index.
   ISBN 0-8368-5038-6 (lib. bdg.)
   ISBN 0-8368-5198-6 (softcover)
   1. Hong Kong (China)—Juvenile literature—Textbooks. [1. Hong Kong
(China)—Textbooks.] I. Title. II. Series.
   DS796.H74B36   2004
   951.25—dc22   2004045524

First published in 2005 by
World Almanac® Library
330 West Olive Street, Suite 100
Milwaukee, WI 53212 USA

Copyright © 2005 by World Almanac® Library.

Produced by Discovery Books
Editor: Kathryn Walker
Series designers: Laurie Shock, Keith Williams
Designer and page production: Ian Winton
Photo researcher: Rachel Tisdale
Diagrams: Keith Williams
Maps and diagrams: Stefan Chabluk
World Almanac® Library editorial direction: Mark J. Sachner
World Almanac® Library editor: Gini Holland
World Almanac® Library art direction: Tammy West
World Almanac® Library graphic design: Scott M. Krall
World Almanac® Library production: Jessica Morris

Photo credits: AKG Images: pp. 8, 11; AKG Images/Paul A. Imasy: p. 12; AKG Images/Jürgen Sorges: p.43; Corbis: pp. 4, 42;
Corbis/Alan Hindle: p. 35; Corbis/David Turnley: p. 27; Corbis Sygma/Patrick Landmann: p. 23; Corbis Sygma/Stephane
Ruet: p. 36; Eye-Ubiquitous/Adina Tovy Amsel: p. 16; Hutchison/Sarah Murray: p. 28; Hutchison/Christine Pemberton:
pp. 18, 30; Chris Fairclough: p.15; James Davis Travel: p. 22; James Davis Worldwide: cover and title page; Reuters: pp. 13,
38; Trip/Keith Cardwell: p. 40; Trip/Colin Conway: pp. 32, 33; Trip/J. Farmer: p. 19; Trip/Jeff Greenberg: p. 20; Trip/Ken
Mclaren: pp. 25, 37; Trip/Jane Sweeney: p. 9, Trip/A. Tovy: pp. 21, 41; Trip/P. Treanor: p. 14; Trip/N. & J. Wiseman: p. 29

Cover caption: Boats in the Causeway Bay Typhoon Shelter with the Wan Chai district of Hong Kong Island in the
background.

Printed in the United States of America

1 2 3 4 5 6 7 8 9 08 07 06 05 04

Contents

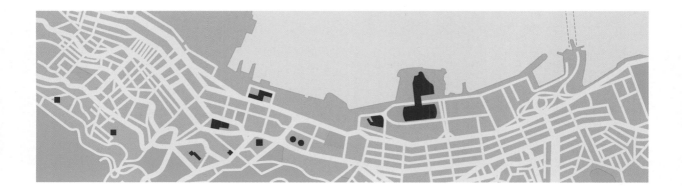

Introduction

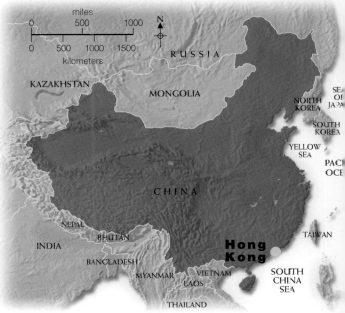

A unique mixture of East and West has made Hong Kong an extraordinary and vibrant city. A British colony from 1841, Hong Kong was handed back to China in 1997, when it officially became a Special Administrative Region (SAR) of China. Hong Kong is a place that never stops, a city where personal progress and making money are the motives that drive everyday life. The hard work, competitiveness, and materialism of its people have fueled Hong Kong's hugely successful economy.

◀ *High-rise buildings define the skyline of Hong Kong Island's Central district, with views across Victoria Harbour to Kowloon.*

Hong Kong is made up of four main areas —the New Territories, Kowloon, Hong Kong Island, and the Outlying Islands. Kowloon and the New Territories lie on a peninsula of the Chinese mainland north of Victoria Harbour. Hong Kong Island rests south of the peninsula, on the south side of Victoria Harbour, while more than 230 other islands are collectively referred to as the Outlying Islands. Hong Kong is a spectacular place, with scenery ranging from the steep wooded hills of Hong Kong Island to the flat, reedy landscape of the Mai Po marshes in the New Territories.

A very small percentage of the land is suitable for building on because the area is so hilly, so high-rise constructions crowd into the sky on Hong Kong Island and Kowloon, with some of the most stunning modern architecture found in Central—the business and financial heart of Hong Kong Island.

"The city appears at the foot of its radiant mountains: It blazes like a great flower of light with stamens and petals of floodlit stone."

—James Kirkup, author, *Streets of Asia*, 1980.

Hong Kong Life

The wealthy tycoons that make up Hong Kong's business elite live in mansions perched on Victoria Peak on Hong Kong Island with fabulous views over Central and Victoria Harbour. For the majority of the

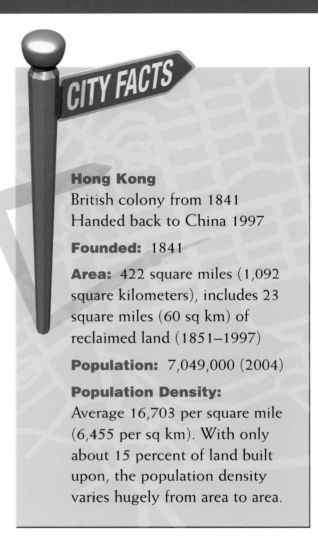

CITY FACTS

Hong Kong
British colony from 1841
Handed back to China 1997

Founded: 1841

Area: 422 square miles (1,092 square kilometers), includes 23 square miles (60 sq km) of reclaimed land (1851–1997)

Population: 7,049,000 (2004)

Population Density:
Average 16,703 per square mile (6,455 per sq km). With only about 15 percent of land built upon, the population density varies hugely from area to area.

population, however, housing is more cramped. Parts of Kowloon have the highest population densities in the world with more than 130,976 people per square mile (50,570 people per square kilometer).

Most of the population of Hong Kong speak Cantonese—a Chinese dialect of the southern province of Guangdong (Canton). English and Cantonese are the official languages but, since the handover in 1997, Mandarin Chinese (the official language of the People's Republic of China) has become more important in Hong Kong.

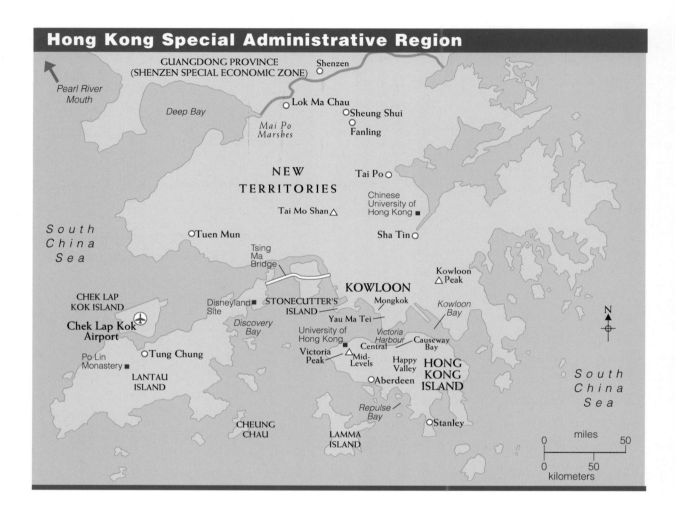

Hong Kong Special Administrative Region

▲ Hong Kong consists of a peninsula of the Chinese mainland and more than 230 islands.

Geography

Hong Kong lies on the southeastern coast of China, on a peninsula in the South China Sea. It has more than 435 miles (700 km) of coastline and a 19-mile (30-km) border with mainland China. Of Hong Kong's various islands, the biggest are Hong Kong Island itself, Lantau, and Lamma. The highest point in Hong Kong is Tai Mo Shan in the New Territories at 3,143 feet (958 meters), but the most famous of its many hills is Victoria Peak at 1,811 feet (552 m) on Hong Kong Island, known simply as "The Peak." Most of Hong Kong is mountainous, except for the lowland areas in the north of the New Territories. Very little of the land —about 5 percent—is used for agriculture, so most of Hong Kong's food is imported.

Wild Hong Kong

A large proportion of Hong Kong's land— about 40 percent—is protected in country parks. There are twenty-three parks,

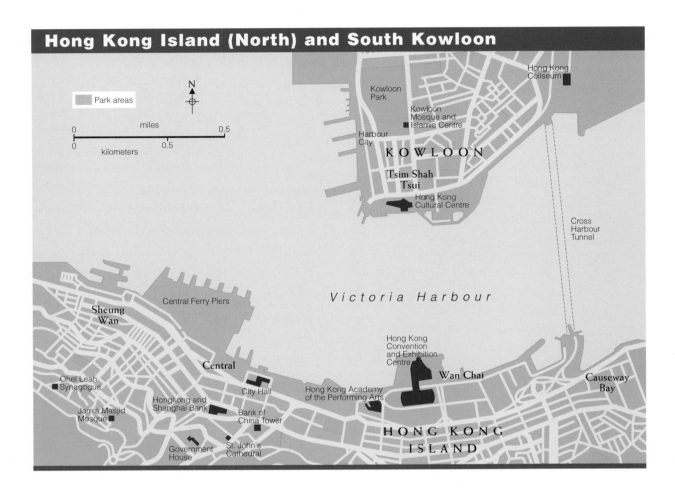

Hong Kong Island (North) and South Kowloon

Park areas

N

miles
0   0.5
0   0.5
kilometers

Hong Kong Coliseum

Kowloon Park

Kowloon Mosque and Islamic Centre

Harbour City

KOWLOON

Tsim Shah Tsui

Hong Kong Cultural Centre

Cross Harbour Tunnel

Victoria Harbour

Central Ferry Piers

Sheung Wan

Hong Kong Convention and Exhibition Centre

Central

Wan Chai

Causeway Bay

Ohel Leah Synagogue

City Hall

Hong Kong Academy of the Performing Arts

Hongkong and Shanghai Bank

Jamia Masjid Mosque

Bank of China Tower

Government House

St. John's Cathedral

HONG KONG ISLAND

including five on Hong Kong Island. The parks include mountainous areas, coasts, woodlands, reservoirs, and islands, providing habitats for a wide variety of animals, birds, and plants.

Climate

Hong Kong has a semi-tropical climate with three main seasons. From October through January or February is the dry season. This is when cold, dry air blows from the northeast bringing cool weather, often with sunny, clear skies. In January, temperatures can dip as low as 50° Fahrenheit (10° Celsius). From

▲ Hong Kong's success was built upon Victoria Harbour, a natural deep-water harbor and today one of the world's busiest waterways.

February on, the temperatures rise, as does the humidity, and there is often fog and drizzle. May through September is the wet season, when the winds bring monsoon rains and the weather is hot and very humid. Sunny days alternate with heavy rain, and in August and September there is a threat of typhoons—big tropical hurricanes or cyclones with winds exceeding seventy-five miles (120 km) per hour.

CHAPTER 1

History of Hong Kong

Evidence of early human habitation dates back to 4000 B.C. in Hong Kong. Archaeological excavations on Lamma, Lantau, and Cheung Chau islands have revealed pottery fragments and evidence of metalworking. Rock carvings have also been found on Hong Kong Island itself. Not surprisingly, these finds have been in coastal sites, suggesting that early inhabitants relied on the sea for food and other supplies. The first migrants from the mainland probably began to arrive during the Qin dynasty (221–206 B.C.) However, we know from the evidence of several sites that imperial rule was extended over the region by the Han dynasty (206 B.C.–A.D. 220). One of these sites was the tomb of a Han warrior, full of Han tomb furniture, found in 1955 in Lei Cheng Uk in Kowloon.

The Five Clans

By the Tang dynasty (A.D. 618–907), the Pearl River had become an important trading link for Arab merchants who sailed up to Guangzhou (Canton), a city port on the Pearl River to the west of Hong Kong, where they

◀ Looking across Victoria Harbour to the dramatic peaks of Hong Kong Island. This picture was painted in 1847, just after Hong Kong became a British colony.

bought silks and pottery. This trade continued to expand during the Song dynasty (960–1279), and it was during this time that Cantonese settlers began to arrive in the fertile valleys and plains of the New Territories. The first of these settlers were members of the Tang clan—a group of people related to each other either by ancestry or marriage. Four other clans followed: the Pang, Hai, Liu, and Man. Together these made up Hong Kong's famous "Five Clans," powerful landowners whose descendants are still there today.

Turbulent Times

In the seventeenth century, devastation came to the region. The Ming dynasty (1368–1644) was overthrown by the Qing (1644–1911). In 1662, the Qing ordered that the population of the whole coastal district, numbering about sixteen thousand, be evacuated inland. This was in order to flush out pirates and Ming rebels. The result was the wholesale destruction of villages and crops, followed by famine. When the area began to be resettled, the government encouraged people from northeast China to move to the region alongside the Cantonese population. They became known as *Hakka*, Cantonese for "guest people."

Trade with the West

In 1557, the Ming emperor allowed Portuguese merchants to establish a trading base at Macau, 40 miles (65 km) west of present-day Hong Kong. From 1685, Guangzhou, also west of Hong Kong,

▲ *Today, some Hakka women still wear their traditional bamboo hats. Fringed with black cloth, the hats protect against insects and the sun.*

became a center of trade with Portuguese, Dutch, and British merchants, mainly for the export of tea, over which China had a world monopoly. Although China was happy to export goods to those referred to as "outer barbarians," the Qing emperors considered China to be self-sufficient and saw no need to import goods from the West. The massive trade imbalance that resulted led the British, among others, to start illegally importing the drug opium into China. Opium addiction quickly swept across China. By 1836, opium was the most expensive commodity in the world.

The Triads

The Triads were originally secret societies founded in China in the seventeenth century with the goal of overthrowing the Qing dynasty and restoring the Ming emperors. (Their motto was "Restore the Ming; overthrow the Qing.") However, during the twentieth century, Triad members increasingly became involved in criminal activities. Today, Triad criminal gangs are active throughout Hong Kong and involved in crimes such as extortion, drug dealing, and robbery.

The Opium Wars

Attempts by China to clamp down on the illegal opium trade led, in 1839, to the First Opium War with Britain. After British warships attacked forts on the Pearl River to the west of Hong Kong Island, China agreed to cede Hong Kong to Britain in perpetuity. The British flag was raised on Hong Kong Island on January 26, 1841. Within months, many Chinese merchants, who had previously lived at Guangzhou and Macau, bought plots of land and moved to Hong Kong Island, where they built offices and warehouses.

In 1856, there was further conflict between China and Britain when Chinese officials boarded a ship flying the British flag to look for pirates and smuggled opium. This led to the Second Opium War, and, by 1858, British and French forces were threatening the Chinese city of Beijing. The war ended with the Treaty of Tianjin, under which China was forced to make more concessions, including ceding the Kowloon peninsula and Stonecutter's Island to the British. In 1898, Britain petitioned China for more land and was granted the lease of the New Territories for ninety-nine years, ending at midnight on June 30, 1997.

"The Chinese will take opium. Only a few chests at first, but the volume of the trade increases at an extraordinary compound rate...."

—Timothy Mo, author, *An Insular Possession*, 1986.

Migrants

When Britain took possession of Hong Kong Island, it had a population of about 3,600 people who lived in small fishing villages on land and another 2,000 people who lived on boats. By 1845, the population had grown to twenty-four thousand, the vast majority being Chinese settlers from the province of Guangdong (Canton).

At first, life in the colony was hard for both Chinese settlers and British colonizers. Malaria, plague, typhoons, piracy, corruption, and lawlessness were just some of the problems that these early settlers faced. There was little communication between the European and Chinese communities and even less understanding. Nevertheless, Hong Kong quickly developed as a port, and, by 1895, it was the fourth largest in the world. The population

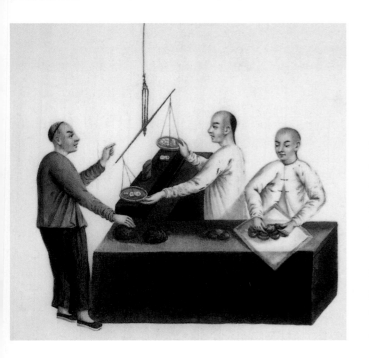

◀ *Chinese traders weigh out opium. The drug was used for pain relief long before opium addiction swept across China in the nineteenth century.*

of the colony also increased, mainly as a result of influxes of political and economic refugees from mainland China. In 1911, the last Chinese emperor was overthrown and the country quickly descended into civil war. There was a steady flow of refugees into Hong Kong throughout these years. When China was invaded by Japan in 1937, hundreds of thousands of people from the Chinese mainland sought refuge in the colony. In 1941, however, Hong Kong was itself occupied by the Japanese. The occupation lasted until the end of World War II, in 1945.

Communist China

By the end of the Japanese occupation, Hong Kong was war ravaged and its population more than halved. Many had fled, but severe food shortages had also caused the Japanese to deport people to ease the strain on such limited supplies. It did not take long, however, for the colony to get back on its feet and for people to rebuild their lives and their businesses. At the same time, hundreds of thousands of exiles and new immigrants poured into the colony. Neighboring China was once again in turmoil as the Nationalists and the Communists struggled for power. On October 1, 1949, the Communist leader Mao Zedong proclaimed the People's Republic of China in Beijing. Many people in Hong Kong expected the Communists to invade, but troops of the People's Liberation Army stopped at the colony's borders.

Recovery and Instability

The events of 1949 in China sent another wave of emigrants across the border into Hong Kong. Some were rich businesspeople, others were peasants and laborers. Hong Kong's economic success of the following years was built upon this mixture of business ability and talent together with cheap labor. Manufacturing became the mainstay of the Hong Kong economy, particularly textiles, plastics, and electronics.

Relations with mainland China remained strained, however, and tensions between Nationalist and Communist sympathizers sometimes brought violence to Hong Kong. There were serious riots in 1956 and 1966.

In 1966, Mao Zedong started a movement known as the Cultural Revolution that encouraged people, the young in particular, to attack the four "olds": old ideas, old culture, old customs, and old habits. In 1967, the chaos of this Cultural Revolution spilled onto Hong Kong's streets with bombs, riots, and anti-British graffiti. (The British government was seen by many as representative of the four "olds.") The situation improved during the 1970s, particularly when the new Chinese leader Deng Xiaoping began to introduce reforms after Mao's death in 1976.

The 1997 Question

During the 1970s and 1980s, Hong Kong became a major financial center. Under

The Last Governor

The last British governor of Hong Kong was Chris Patten. While previous governors had been diplomats specializing in Chinese matters, Patten was a politician. He was appointed in 1992, a crucial time in Hong Kong's history because of the soon-to-come handover. He announced plans to introduce electoral reform for greater democracy that were passed by the Legislative Council (the body responsible for passing laws). However, these plans drew immediate criticism from Beijing, and relations with China remained strained until the handover of Hong Kong to China in 1997.

Deng Xiaoping's reforms, China opened its doors to tourism, trade, and foreign investment, and Hong Kong became the gateway for business with China. Investment poured into Hong Kong and the colony flourished. People began to ask questions, however, about what would happen in 1997, when the lease of the New Territories ran out. It was not practical for Britain to try to keep Hong Kong and Kowloon without the populous New Territories, so negotiations (begun between Britain and China in the late 1970s) had to be about the whole colony. In 1984, China and Britain announced that Hong Kong

◀ *The various forms of transportation, seen here in the 1950s on a wet day in Central, included streetcars and rickshaws (small covered carriages pulled by men).*

would be handed back to China in 1997, as originally agreed. The prospect of Chinese rule, which would replace democracy and capitalism with communism, caused many people to emigrate from the colony.

▲ The Chinese and British flags hang side by side during the handover ceremony in 1997. The line-up of people at the front includes the new Chief Executive of Hong Kong, Tung Chee-Hwa (left), and the outgoing governor of Hong Kong, Chris Patten (second from right).

The "Handover"

On the night of June 30, 1997, the last British governor of Hong Kong formally handed the colony back to China. The man appointed by Beijing to take over as chief executive was a business tycoon, Tung Chee-Hwa. He was appointed for five years and re-elected for a second term in 2002. The compromise agreed to by the UK and China for the handover was that Hong Kong would continue its capitalist system and way of life for fifty years. For that length of time, China agreed not to impose its communist economic or political systems on the former colony. Under this agreement, Hong Kong became a Special Administrative Region (SAR) of China.

People of Hong Kong

Throughout its history, Hong Kong has been a magnet for immigrants. The vast majority of the population of Hong Kong—about 98 percent—is Chinese. About 70 percent of these people are immigrants or children of immigrants from Guangdong province in southern China. Many consider themselves to be Hong Kong rather than Chinese citizens. Nevertheless, Canton Chinese traditions, language, and cuisine are an integral part of Hong Kong culture.

Other Chinese groups in Hong Kong include immigrants from coastal regions such as Shanghai and Fuzhou, as well as the Hakka, Hoklo, and Tanka people. The Hakka ("guest people") have been landowners in Hong Kong since the late seventeenth century, mainly in the New Territories. Traditionally, Hakka women are forbidden from inheriting land, so it is passed down through sons and kept in the family. Many Hakkas work as farmers, but Hakkas also control many of the stone quarrying and bean curd industries in Hong Kong. The Hoklo and Tanka are "boat people" who used to live on houseboat "junks" (Chinese vessels) in Aberdeen on Hong Kong Island, Yau Ma Tei in

◀ *Streets are often busy along Hong Kong Island's Causeway Bay.*

► *A community of Tanka people still live aboard their boats in Aberdeen Harbour and make a living from fishing.*

Kowloon, and other harbors. Most have now come ashore to live and work, although some junks still remain in Aberdeen. The Hoklo were fishers who originated in Fuzhou province in southern China. The Tanka may be descended from some of the earliest people to have settled the south Chinese coast.

Vietnamese Boat People

From the late 1970s, thousands of refugees made the journey from war-torn Vietnam across the East China Sea to Hong Kong. More than 200,000 of these "boat people" reached the colony and were housed in refugee camps. Many were sent back to their homeland; some were resettled overseas; and thousands were given asylum in Hong Kong itself.

Foreign Communities

The largest of the foreign communities living in Hong Kong is made up of people from the Philippines, mostly women. More than 100,000 Filipinas (women from the Philippines) work in Hong Kong, mainly as domestic staff. Although some are highly qualified, with university degrees, they come to Hong Kong for comparatively menial employment because they can earn much more here than in the Philippines. Many save as much as possible from their salaries to send home to their families. Every Sunday, thousands of Filipinas congregate in the public squares of Central to meet friends and relax. Hong Kong also has Thai, Japanese, Indonesian, and Indian populations. Western expatriates (known in Cantonese as *gweilo*, meaning "foreign devils") come from Canada, the United States, Britain, and Australia. Most work in the businesses that are based in Hong Kong.

"Make the local people happy and attract migrants from afar."

—Confucius, philosopher, *The Analects of Confucius,* c. 500 B.C.

Religions

Given the multicultural population of Hong Kong, it isn't surprising that there is a wide range of religions in the city. For the Chinese population, the main religions are the traditional Chinese beliefs of Daoism, Buddhism, Confucianism, and ancestor worship. There are also sizable populations of Christians, Muslims, Jews, and Hindus in Hong Kong.

Chinese Beliefs

The beliefs of Daoism, Buddhism, and Confucianism shape the lives of most of the Hong Kong Chinese population. *Dao* means the "way" or "path," and Daoists believe that dao provides a guiding principle for truth and life. Daoism is a native Chinese religion whose founder, Laozi, is said to have lived during the sixth century B.C. Buddhism began in India and was introduced to China during the first century A.D. It spread throughout China between the third and sixth centuries, when several distinct schools of Chinese Buddhism developed. Buddhists use meditation to strive for the ultimate truth of existence. Confucianism is a philosophy concerning the ordering of human relations, stressing the importance of family and social ties. It is derived from the teachings of a Chinese wise man, Confucius (c. 551–479 B.C.)

In practice, most Hong Kong Chinese people take as practical a view of religion as

▼ *A huge Buddha statue, "Big Buddha," overlooks the Po Lin Monastery on Lantau Island.*

Local Gods and Goddesses

Some gods and goddesses have become associated with particular places or groups of people in Hong Kong.

Kwan Kung: god of war who eventually became known as the god of wealth, also patron of the police force and the Triads.

Kwun Yum: goddess of mercy and patron of all

Tin Hau: goddess of heaven and protector of fishers.

Tsai Shin: god of riches and patron of storekeepers.

Wong Tai Sin: patron of an area in North Kowloon, also of businesspeople and the sick.

Pak Tai: patron of Cheung Chau.

they do of most other aspects of life. Many follow both the Daoist and Buddhist faiths; they tend to be less concerned with the spiritual aspects of these faiths than with practical requests for good luck, wealth, and health. People go to the temples to take gifts, burn incense, and make supplications (pray for good fortune). Great importance is also placed on the worship of dead ancestors. Frequent offerings of food and incense are made at small altars that contain ancestor tablets—small blocks inscribed with the dead person's name.

Places of Worship

There are about half a million Christians in Hong Kong, with the main centers of worship at St. John's Cathedral for Anglicans (followers of the Church of England) and St. Joseph's for Catholics, both on Hong Kong Island. There are also Baptist, Lutheran, and Methodist churches. About half of the eighty thousand or so Muslims in Hong Kong are Chinese. The remainder come from the Indian, Indonesian, and other communities. The oldest mosque is the Jamia Masjid in Kowloon, founded in the late nineteenth century. A more recent mosque is the Kowloon Mosque and Islamic Center at Tsim Sha Tsui. Many of Hong Kong's community of Jews worship at the Ohel Leah Synagogue in the Mid-Levels on Hong Kong Island, while Hindus have an impressive temple in Happy Valley, also on Hong Kong Island. In contrast to the Chinese mainland, there is complete freedom of worship in Hong Kong.

Festivals

Many traditional Chinese festivals are celebrated in Hong Kong, ranging from the island Cheung Chau's unique Bun Festival (a celebration that honors the Daoist god of the sea and seeks to drive evil spirits away) to the two-thousand-year-old Dragon Boat Festival. Hong Kong also has public holidays to mark the Christian celebrations of Easter and Christmas. Since the handover to China in 1997, three new public holidays have entered the calendar: Labor Day (May 1), Hong Kong SAR Establishment Day (July 1), and China National Day (October 1 and 2).

Family Occasions

The most important holiday festival time is the Chinese New Year, which falls some time between January 21 and February 19, depending on the lunar calendar. During this three-day public holiday, shops and businesses shut and families get together. It is also a time for settling arguments and paying debts. The most common New Year greeting in Hong Kong is *kung hei fat choi*, which literally translated means "good wishes, get rich." Children and unmarried adults receive *laisee*, small red envelopes containing money in fresh new bills. The skyscrapers in Central are lit up with lights for the festival and there is a spectacular fireworks display in Victoria Harbour on the evening of the second day.

Another family festival is *Ching Ming*, meaning "bright and clear," which is when

▲ *A dragon boat race takes place in Aberdeen Harbour as part of the Dragon Boat Festival.*

families visit the graves of their ancestors. They clean the graves and give offerings of incense, food, clothing, and money; then they enjoy a family picnic. In the New Territories, more formal rituals take place at the graves of members of the Five Clans.

Colorful Celebrations

Some of the most colorful public celebrations in Hong Kong are on the water. In June, the Dragon Boat Festival is held in harbors all around Hong Kong. Painted boats up to 100 feet (30 m) long and with as many as fifty rowers race against each other. The most spectacular races are held in Victoria Harbour. In late April or early May, the Hoklo and Tanka people

The Bun Festival

Unique to Hong Kong is the Bun Festival, which is held on the island of Cheung Chau in late April or early May. It is a Daoist festival dedicated to the god Pak Tai, who is believed to have driven away evil spirits from the island. During the festival, three huge towers of rice flour buns are erected, mounted on 65-foot- (20-meter-) high bamboo and paper scaffolding (see below). In the past, young men scrambled up the towers on the last day of the festival to reach the highest bun, but after an incident in 1978, when a tower collapsed and several people were injured, the buns are now handed out to the waiting crowds. The Bun Festival also features performances of Chinese opera and spectacular processions.

celebrate the birthday of the sea goddess, Tin Hau. They decorate their boats with colorful silk banners and sail to her temples to pray for protection at sea.

Food

Eating is a major social activity in Hong Kong—the local greeting is "Have you eaten?" Much of the housing in the city is so cramped that many people eat out at least once a day. Food of all nationalities can be eaten in Hong Kong, but, as the majority of the population comes from Guangdong (Canton) province, the main cuisine of

"Food is heaven."

—Ancient Chinese proverb.

Hong Kong is Cantonese. Many other Chinese cuisines are also popular, including Chiu Chow, Shanghainese, Sichuan, and northern Chinese—each with its own distinctive flavor.

Cantonese Food

The main characteristic of Cantonese cooking is the freshness of the ingredients. Many Chinese people shop two or three times a day to ensure that the food they cook is as fresh as possible. Restaurant owners often maintain tanks full of live fish that their cooks select, cook, and then serve immediately. Their main methods of cooking are steaming and stir-frying in hot oil, in a type of deeply slope-sided frying pan called a

wok. They enhance the delicate flavors of their fish, seafood, chicken, pork, and vegetables with a wide range of sauces.

Meals in Hong Kong are often social and noisy occasions, typically starting with an appetizer of barbecued meat. All the main course food is placed in the center of the table and people help themselves with chopsticks from communal dishes. Hong Kong diners often end their meals with soup, which they eat with porcelain spoons. They usually enjoy tea served with the meal in small, handleless cups.

▼ *In Hong Kong, people often buy snacks at open-air food stalls, where they find a range of traditional fast food (shown here). Many also eat Western-style fast food.*

Other Cuisines

Hong Kong's history as a British colony and an international commercial center is reflected in the wide variety of food available in the city—it is possible to eat at restaurants offering British, French, Greek, Italian, Indian, Thai, Japanese, and Swiss food. The other Chinese cuisines (apart from Cantonese) reflect the traditions of the minority Chinese populations in Hong Kong. Shanghainese food is rich and oily; Sichuan is spicy; Chiu Chow food is often served with a thick, soupy rice called congee; while northern Chinese food is served with noodles and steamed bread. The Hakka also have their own eating traditions—two of their best-known dishes are stuffed duck and salt-baked chicken.

Dim Sum

Dim sum (pictured above) *is a Cantonese specialty and a vital part of everyday life for many Hong Kong Chinese. Dim sum means "touching the heart," and it refers to small, steamed dumplings filled with a wide variety of stuffings, as well as spring rolls, small buns, tarts, pastries, and cakes. Steamed dim sum are usually served in small bamboo baskets; other dim sum are deep-fried. Dim sum is eaten for breakfast or lunch (not in the evening). On the weekends, dim sum restaurants are packed with families and friends. Dim sum is typically served by waiters who bring their diners an array of choices from table to table at frequent intervals.*

CHAPTER 3

Living in Hong Kong

Throughout the twentieth century, the waves of immigrants coming into Hong Kong, mainly from the Chinese mainland, put great strains on housing. Squatter settlements grew up to accommodate the new arrivals. These were settlements of huts that appeared on land that was unsuitable for normal building development. It was in one of these settlements, at Shek Kip Mei in northern Kowloon, that fire broke out on Christmas Eve, 1953. The fire raged overnight, and, by Christmas Day, 53,000 people were homeless. Forced to act, the Hong Kong government began a housing program to resettle the fire victims. This was the beginning of what was to become the largest public housing program in the world.

The goal of Hong Kong's Housing Authority, founded in 1954, was to provide reasonable and affordable permanent housing for all residents of Hong Kong. Today, half the population lives in permanent public housing. The amount paid in rent, or to buy a flat, is partly determined by the amount the tenant can afford.

◀ *A housing development in Sha Tin, in the New Territories. Sha Tin is one of the oldest of the new towns, built in the 1970s on reclaimed land.*

New Towns

The mountainous geography of much of Hong Kong makes it difficult to build on most of the land. In fact, only about 15 percent of the total land area of Hong Kong is built upon. In the areas where it is possible to build, developers make the most of the space. The average amount of space per person in public housing is 36 square feet (11 sq m), and, by Western standards, most Hong Kong apartments are extremely cramped. In an attempt to ease the overcrowding in central areas, the Hong Kong government has put money into reclaiming land for development. Another solution has been to build new towns in the New Territories. It has been vital to provide opportunities for employment and efficient transportation links to these towns, where

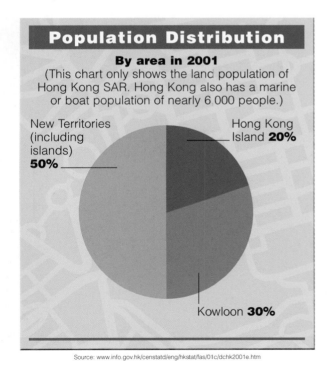

Population Distribution

By area in 2001

(This chart only shows the land population of Hong Kong SAR. Hong Kong also has a marine or boat population of nearly 6 000 people.)

New Territories (including islands) **50%**

Hong Kong Island **20%**

Kowloon **30%**

Source: www.info.gov.hk/censtatd/eng/hkstat/fas/01c/dchk2001e.htm

Cage Dwellers

For those Hong Kong citizens living on low incomes—particularly for older single people—it can be very difficult to find good, affordable accommodations. In Mongkok in Kowloon, some people rent "cages" (pictured above) to live and sleep in. These are found in apartments that have been partitioned into rows of bed spaces, stacked one above the other, in two or three tiers. Often, wire mesh surrounds the units to protect the lodgers' belongings, giving the appearance of rows of cages. A unit is about 3 feet (1m) square and 6.5 feet (2m) long. Occupants share bathroom and kitchen facilities. Some residents have lived in these cramped conditions for as long as thirty or forty years.

more than 40 percent of the population of Hong Kong now live.

Despite all these measures to accommodate its population, Hong Kong still has problems of homelessness and squatter developments. Some people sleep out on the streets, in underpasses, and shop doorways.

Feng Shui

The ancient art of feng shui ("wind and water") is taken very seriously in Hong Kong. Feng shui is the art of living in harmony with the natural world. When people in Hong Kong plan new buildings, or before a family moves in to a new home, they consult a feng shui expert about the direction the building should face, or where they should position their furniture. The Hongkong and Shanghai Bank building in Central is said to have excellent feng shui. Almost next door, the Bank of China building, with its sharp edges and acute angles, is said to have bad feng shui and to send out "secret arrows" aimed at the old Government House up the hill. This is one reason the Chief Executive of Hong Kong, Tung Chee-hwa, gave for not moving into Government House after the 1997 handover.

"Even today, no Hong Kong employer, from the richest bank to the simplest corner store, can afford to ignore the precepts [principles] of Wind and Water."

—Jan Morris, author, Hong Kong: *Epilogue to Empire,* 1988.

Shops and Markets

Hong Kong is known worldwide as a major shopping center, and shopping is a favorite pastime of Hong Kong citizens and tourists alike. From shops selling designer luxury labels in glamorous malls to stalls in bustling, noisy markets, Hong Kong has a huge variety of shopping outlets.

▼ *Customers browse among the stacked cages at the Bird Market in Mongkok, Kowloon. The Chinese like to keep birds, and especially songbirds, as pets.*

The main shopping areas are Central and Causeway Bay on Hong Kong Island and Tsim Shah Tsui in Kowloon. All three areas have huge shopping malls. For example, the Landmark in Central and the vast Harbour City in Tsim Shah Tsui offer shoppers more than six hundred stores. Causeway Bay is known by locals as "little Japan," because it has Japanese department stores and stores selling Japanese electrical goods.

Hong Kong's reputation as a shopping haven is linked to its world importance as a port and as a manufacturing center. Goods that have been manufactured in Hong Kong can be bought much more cheaply there than elsewhere. It is also possible to buy imported goods at lower prices because Hong Kong does not charge duty, sales tax, or import taxes. Tourists and Hong Kong citizens look for bargains in clothes, jewelry, watches, cameras, computers, and other electrical goods.

There are many other areas in Hong Kong for shoppers, but for a different kind of shopping experience there are the numerous markets that sell everything from fish to jade. Kowloon provides the Jade Market and the Temple Market—a busy night market with entertainers, fortune tellers, food stalls, and Chinese opera shows. Kowloon also houses the Mongkok Bird Market, where cages full of songbirds are stacked high, and the nearby Flower Market. Hong Kong Island hosts a market where vendors sell cheap clothes, shoes, and household goods at Stanley and

Counterfeits and Fakes

Hong Kong has a worldwide reputation as a center for shopping, but it also has a reputation as a center for the sale of counterfeits and fakes. Fake designer watches and clothes, bootleg CDs and tapes, and many other counterfeit goods are widely available in stores and markets throughout Hong Kong. Often, the only clue for the purchaser is a suspiciously low price for a well-known "name." The Hong Kong Tourist Board became so worried about the damage being done to the tourist trade by the sale of fakes that it has introduced a plan to identify shops that offer a reliable service.

also at the Western Market at Sheung Wan, which is housed in a large red-brick building dating from 1906.

Education

Since the 1970s, education in Hong Kong has been compulsory for nine years—six years in elementary school, from age six until age eleven, followed by three years of junior secondary school (junior high school). The curriculum in elementary school includes Chinese, English, math, social studies, science, health education, music, physical education, and arts and crafts. Many children attend kindergarten before elementary school, and most stay on for an extra two years at senior secondary school (high school), which leads them to the first public examination, the Hong Kong Certificate of Education Examination (HKCEE). Following the HKCEE (the non-compulsory two-year course of study known as "sixth-form"), students may choose between art, science, or business subjects and prepare for the Hong Kong Advanced Level Examination (HKALE). After this, students may go on to university, either to study for a degree or for vocational training such as teacher training.

A Question of Language

In most elementary schools in Hong Kong (except for international schools), the curriculum is taught in Cantonese. However, secondary education has traditionally been taught in both Cantonese and English. English is still important in Hong Kong as the language of finance and trade, so most parents want their children to learn it. Therefore, there was an outcry after the 1997 handover, when the Chinese government told most secondary schools to change to teaching exclusively in Cantonese. A compromise was reached: The schools continued to teach some lessons in English, and English remains a core requirement for university entrance. Other changes after the handover included new subjects in the curriculum, such as Mandarin (the official language of the People's Republic of China) and the study of the Basic Law (the laws on which the government of Hong Kong is based).

Higher Education

Of the eight universities in Hong Kong, the oldest and most prestigious is the University of Hong Kong. It opened in 1887 as a medical school and was officially founded in 1911. The university campus lies on the western side of Hong Kong Island in Pok Fu Lam. The Chinese University of Hong Kong and the Hong Kong University of Science and Technology are both in the

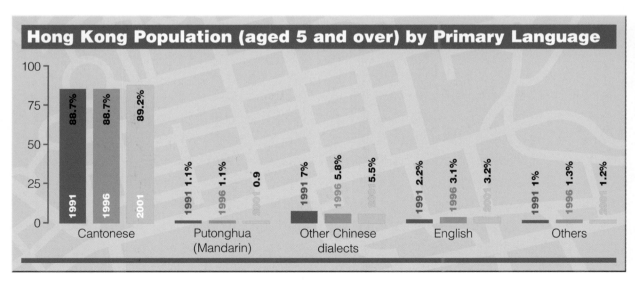

Hong Kong Population (aged 5 and over) by Primary Language

Cantonese: 1991 88.7%, 1996 88.7%, 2001 89.2%
Putonghua (Mandarin): 1991 1.1%, 1996 1.1%, 2001 0.9
Other Chinese dialects: 1991 7%, 1996 5.8%, 2001 5.5%
English: 1991 2.2%, 1996 3.1%, 2001 3.2%
Others: 1991 1%, 1996 1.3%, 2001 1.2%

▲ *A student at a Hong Kong school. About 18 percent of students go on to study at university.*

Sun Yat-sen (1866-1925)

One of the most famous people to have attended the University of Hong Kong was Sun Yat-sen, often referred to as father of the Republic of China. He studied in Honolulu, Hawaii, before earning a medical degree in Hong Kong and working as a doctor in the colony. He was determined to fight the backwardness and corruption of the Chinese Qing dynasty, and after the overthrow of the emperor, in 1911, he was declared the first (provisional) president of the Republic of China, although he quickly stepped down from the post.

New Territories. The Chinese University was opened in 1963, the University of Science and Technology in 1991. All three have worldwide reputations for excellence. Other local universities include the City University, the Hong Kong Baptist University, and the Lingnan University.

"Where did I get my Revolutionary ideas? It was entirely in Hong Kong."

—Sun Yat-sen, first president of the Republic of China, 1922.

27

Transportation

Hong Kong has an efficient and cheap public transportation system that allows people to travel around Hong Kong with great ease. There are many methods of travel—ferry, subway, train, bus, minibus, streetcar, and even a funicular railway on Hong Kong Island which pulls people up the steep hillside from Central to Victoria Peak. Several road and rail tunnels connect Hong Kong Island and Kowloon, running beneath the sea bed of Victoria Harbour.

Old and New

The old airport, called Kai Tak, was built in Kowloon with its runway extending into Hong Kong Harbour. It gave one of the most

▲ *The glass walls of Chek Lap Kok, Hong Kong's new international airport, encourage visitors to enjoy spectacular views of the surrounding sea.*

heart-stopping descents in the world as planes flew low over the high-rise buildings below. Hong Kong's new airport at Chek Lap Kok opened in 1998 and has three times the capacity of Kai Tak, handling up to eighty-seven million passengers per year. The airport was a major engineering undertaking that involved a huge land reclamation project and flattening a small island off Lantau. It is connected to Kowloon and Hong Kong Island by a high-speed rail link and by freeways that run across Tsing Ma, one of the world's longest suspension bridges.

Getting Around

Since the handover in 1997, overland travel from Hong Kong to mainland China has become much easier, with good bus and train services. Boats and ferries also link Hong Kong to destinations on the Chinese mainland. The Mass Transit Railway (MTR) is a fast and efficient subway system that connects all parts of Hong Kong. The system has clean, air-conditioned stations and trains and gets very busy at peak times. For more traditional travel, streetcars run on 10 miles (16 km) of track through Central on Hong Kong Island while the famous Star

The Peak Tram

This funicular railway, or cable-run railway, known as the Peak tram, is the steepest in the world. Although it attracts many tourists, it is used daily as a practical means of transportation by local people who need to travel up and down Victoria Peak. Built in 1888, it has never had an accident. It has two cars that balance one another as one is pulled up and the other lowered by 5,000-foot (1,500-m) steel cables wound around drums at the top. The two cars pass on one small section of double track in the middle.

Ferry connects Hong Kong Island and Kowloon. Double-decker buses and minibuses transport people all over Hong Kong, as do air-conditioned taxis.

Problems

Historically, Hong Kong has had a policy of minimal control over the activities of businesses, putting the importance of economic growth above other concerns. The strain this policy has put on Hong Kong's environment has become clear in recent years, however, as Hong Kong Island is regularly shrouded in smog (a smoky fog), and Victoria Harbour has become increasingly polluted. Since this impacts health, quality of life, and the business of tourism, environmental issues are now high on the political agenda of Hong Kong citizens. Steps are now being taken to address the main problem areas.

Air and Water Pollution

Air quality began to deteriorate in Hong Kong during the 1970s and 1980s, mainly as a result

▼ Windsurfers on a beach on Cheung Chau. Tourism is very important to Hong Kong's economy, so the water quality on the beaches is carefully monitored and controlled.

of emissions from industry and power plants. During the 1990s, however, the amount of traffic on Hong Kong's roads increased dramatically—by about 25 percent. Emissions from vehicles became the major source of the smog that regularly clouds Hong Kong's skies. One problem was that more than 60 percent of all vehicles ran on diesel fuel, which pumps tiny particulates into the air. Solutions include providing incentives for taxis and buses to switch to Liquid Petroleum Gas (LPG) and fitting diesel-powered vehicles with devices that reduce their emissions. The government has tightened controls over smoky vehicles and gives out stiff fines for offenders.

Much of the raw sewage (about 70 percent) that used to pour into Victoria Harbour is now being treated at a new plant on Stonecutter's Island before being released into the water. This has helped to improve the water quality, but many problems still need to be addressed—not least of which is the 30 percent of raw sewage that still goes directly into the water. The problems are not confined to Victoria Harbour: As more towns are built in the New Territories, water pollution is becoming an issue in these areas, too.

Noise

In a location with some of the highest population densities in the world, it is not surprising that noise pollution is a day-to-day problem for many Hong Kong residents. Noise from building work, traffic, and air conditioning plants cause much of it. To combat this, more controls are being placed on construction work, and plans to create traffic-free zones are being employed in some residential areas to reduce noise levels. One major source of noise pollution has been removed, however. People under the flight path into Kai Tak airport used to live with the regular scream of aircraft engines overhead. Some teachers were forced to address their classes through megaphones. In comparison, noise from the new airport affects very few people because of its location and altered flight paths.

"Hong Kong is non-stop noise: clanking jack-hammers, bleeping pagers and mobile phones, clanking mah-jong sets, roaring traffic, clanging trams [streetcars], hooting ships."

—Chris Patten, former and last Governor of Hong Kong and author, *East and West*, 1998.

Illegal Trade

All kinds of goods come into and go out of Hong Kong. Some of the most exotic are used in Chinese medicine or cuisine. Delicacies such as shark fins are traded legally, but other substances, including rhino horn and tiger bones —both used in traditional Chinese cures—are illegal. This trade threatens species that are almost on the point of extinction, but interest in Chinese medicine is growing and demand for these products remains high.

CHAPTER 4

Hong Kong at Work

Hong Kong has a limited supply of land and virtually no land-based natural resources. It has, however, an excellent deep-water port—the container port at Kwai Chung is the busiest in the world—and a location that makes it a world center for imports and exports. It also has a population willing to work long and hard for success. All these factors have helped make Hong Kong one of the world's largest trading economies.

A Recipe for Success

There are also other reasons for Hong Kong's business success. For many years, Hong Kong has prided itself on its free market. The Hong Kong government has interfered as little as possible in the running of companies, while providing a good business environment. Taxation is low—16.5 percent on company profits and no more than 15 percent on personal incomes. There is a sound legal and financial framework in Hong Kong and there are strong anti-corruption laws. Communications within Hong Kong are good and customs procedures for import

◄ *The spectacular Bank of China building was designed by the Chinese American architect I. M. Pei and stands 1,209 feet (368 m) high*

and export are straightforward. Add to these factors Hong Kong's skilled and enterprising work force, and you have the recipe for Hong Kong's success.

Many people pay the price for this success, however. People often work in cramped and dangerous conditions, with no access to trade unions or any form of representation. They have no minimum wage, and many have to work long hours just to make ends meet—some up to seventy hours per week. For those without work (about 7 percent of the population) social welfare provides only the most basic help. Yet Hong Kong remains a

▲ *A huge container ship docked at the Kwai Chung Container Terminal in the western New Territories.*

place of opportunity for ambitious and productive workers.

Manufacturing

The enterprising spirit of the immigrants that flooded into Hong Kong from China in 1949 sparked a new era of manufacturing in the colony. At first, manufacturing was based around textiles and clothes—still the largest industrial employer in Hong Kong —but manufacturers soon expanded to include toys, plastic products, electronics, watches and clocks, and photographic equipment. Manufacturing has become less important in recent years, partly because many companies have relocated to mainland China to find cheaper labor. At the same time, service industries (industries that provide a service rather than a manufactured product) have become more dominant. Industry now accounts for about 13 percent of Hong Kong's Gross Domestic Product (GDP)—the value of all the goods and services the region produces in a year.

Finance and Business

Service industries—business, finance, telecommunications, insurance, tourism—account for about 86 percent of GDP in Hong Kong today. Before the late 1970s, business was dominated by British companies, known as *hongs*, such as Jardine Matheson, Hutchison Whampoa, and Swire. Some of them dated back to 1841,

when Hong Kong first became a British colony. During the 1980s, however, many Hong Kong Chinese set up rival business empires, often dealing with mainland China. Today, Hong Kong is the world's fifth-largest banking center, with over eighty of the world's top one hundred banks having headquarters there.

Links with China

Under the leadership of Mao Zedong (1949–1976), China had little trade with other countries. With the exception of aid from the Soviet Union, a fellow communist state, China received no foreign investment during this time. However, Mao's successor, Deng Xiaoping, started to put in place economic reforms in the late 1970s. The Hong Kong business community was quick to take advantage of the changes, and since that time their links between Hong Kong and the mainland have been vitally important. Hong Kong became the

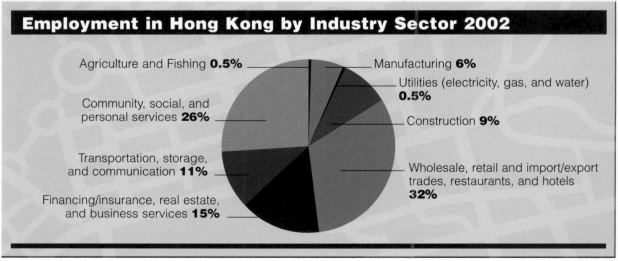

Employment in Hong Kong by Industry Sector 2002

Agriculture and Fishing **0.5%**

Community, social, and personal services **26%**

Transportation, storage, and communication **11%**

Financing/insurance, real estate, and business services **15%**

Manufacturing **6%**

Utilities (electricity, gas, and water) **0.5%**

Construction **9%**

Wholesale, retail and import/export trades, restaurants, and hotels **32%**

Source: www.info.gov.hk/censtatd/eng/hkstat/hkin/labour/labor5.htm

gateway for trade between the vast market of China and the rest of the world.

Since the handover in 1997, Hong Kong's status as a Special Administrative Region has allowed it to remain separate from mainland China in all matters other than foreign affairs and defense, at least until 2047. Today, China is Hong Kong's largest trading partner. About 40 percent of the goods traded in Hong Kong are exports to or imports from China. Links with Guangdong province have become particularly strong since 1997, with many companies taking advantage of the improved communications between the mainland and Hong Kong.

"As long as we move with the times, play to our strengths, the strategic position and unique role of Hong Kong cannot be replaced."

—Tung Chee-hwa, chief executive of Hong Kong, 2003.

Crashes and Crises

Just after the handover in 1997, Hong Kong was affected by a financial crash that hit economies across East Asia. The crisis sent Hong Kong into recession for the first time in years, causing many people to lose their jobs. The Hong Kong government put together a rescue package, and Hong Kong gradually recovered. In 2003, however, another crisis hit the city—an epidemic of a pneumonia virus known as Severe Acute

SARS Epidemic

This terrifying illness originated in southern China in November 2002. The first case was reported in Hong Kong in February 2003; in March the SARS (Severe Acute Respiratory Syndrome) epidemic forced the government to close schools throughout Hong Kong and send more than one thousand people into quarantine. In April, the World Health Organization advised people not to visit Hong Kong unless absolutely necessary. Hong Kong was declared free of SARS on June 23, 2003, but by that time great damage had already been done to the economy. The number of tourists to Hong Kong dropped dramatically, with a corresponding effect on hotels, shops, restaurants, and other entertainment, while business confidence also suffered.

Respiratory Syndrome (SARS). Hong Kong's economy stumbled once again, but the long-term effects of the crisis remain to be seen.

"One country, two systems."

—Slogan summing up the Hong Kong handover agreement between the UK and China.

Government

The government of Hong Kong is made up of a Legislative Council (often referred to as Legco) and an Executive Council. The Legislative Council is responsible for passing laws proposed by the Executive Council. It also approves budgets, taxation, and public expenditure, and monitors government work. The fourteen members of the Executive Council are usually civil servants, and they advise the chief executive (appointed by Beijing) on policy-making. Both the government of Hong Kong and the judiciary (judges) are governed by the Basic Law—a set of laws drawn up as part of the handover agreement and published in 1988 by Beijing. In addition, there are eighteen district boards that deal with local issues.

▲ *Tung Chee-Hwa is a shipping tycoon who was appointed by the Beijing government to be Hong Kong's first chief executive after the handover in 1997.*

The Bauhinia Flower

When Hong Kong was a British colony, the Union Jack (the British flag) fluttered from the top of flagpoles and the British monarch's face appeared on its coins. After the handover to China, these symbols of colonial power were replaced not with the Chinese flag, but with a new design. The official symbol of Hong Kong is a white bauhinia flower on a red background, with the five stars of the Chinese flag on its five petals. This is the symbol that now appears on Hong Kong's coins and on its flags. The bauhinia, also known as the Hong Kong Orchid Tree, is an evergreen plant with mauve flowers that is unique to Hong Kong.

The members of the Executive Council are appointed by the chief executive, but members of the Legislative Council are elected. The Legislative Council has sixty members. In the 2000 elections, twenty-four members were elected by the people of Hong Kong and thirty members by "functional constituencies" (groups defined by their occupation and mostly dominated by the business community). Six members were elected by an eight-hundred-strong Election Committee, mostly made up of Beijing interests. Political parties in Hong Kong include the Democratic Party, the Liberal Party, and the Democratic Alliance for the Betterment of Hong Kong. The Democratic Party won much of the popular vote in the 2000 elections, but because of the rules of appointment, it remains a minority party in the Legislative Council.

▼ *The Hong Kong Legislative Council meets in the old Supreme Court building in Central, Hong Kong Island. It was built in 1915.*

CHAPTER 5

Hong Kong at Play

Hong Kong has a vibrant nightlife, with huge numbers of bars and clubs playing music that ranges from salsa to garage. Hong Kong also enjoys a very active cultural scene, with a great variety of theater, music, and film, all of which draw on both Chinese and Western traditions.

Classical Music

The Hong Kong Philharmonic Orchestra is a Western-style orchestra that performs Western classical music as well as music by local composers. The Hong Kong Chinese Orchestra plays traditional Chinese music and Western music on Chinese instruments.

Cantopop

From the late 1970s, pop songs written in Cantonese began to be popular in Hong Kong. Promoted by the movie star Sam Hui, these songs reflected the concerns and lives of people in the colony. The first "Cantopop" stars came to fame during the 1980s and at the start of the 1990s. Four of these stars—Leon Lai, Jackie Cheung, Aaron Kwok, and Andy Lau—were declared the "Four Heavenly Kings" of Cantopop. Since then other stars have taken over, including the singer Faye Wong (pictured left).

Both have their home at the Hong Kong Cultural Centre in Tsim Sha Tsui and also perform at City Hall on the other side of Victoria Harbour. The Hong Kong Academy of the Performing Arts (HKAPA), one of the top performing arts schools in Asia, is a source of talented young musicians for these orchestras.

Dance

Dance is an important part of cultural life in Hong Kong, and the HKAPA again plays a vital role, providing expert training for local dancers, some of whom go on to have international careers. The Hong Kong Ballet performs classical and modern ballet both at home and on tour. The Hong Kong Dance Company performs Chinese dance in traditional, folk, and modern styles, while other dance companies specialize in modern dance.

Arts Festivals

Hong Kong hosts a number of festivals that draw big names from all around the world. Residents enjoy annual festivals such as the Hong Kong Arts Festival (featuring theater, art, and dance events); the Fringe Festival (a showcase for experimental theater); and the Hong Kong Film Festival. The Festival of Asian Arts is held every other year. Hong Kong attracts some major international pop artists, but Cantopop provides residents with their own local heart throbs. Venues for live music include the Hong Kong Coliseum and the Queen Elizabeth Stadium.

Opera

While it is possible to see performances of Western operas at the HKAPA, Chinese opera is the form that is most loved by the people of Hong Kong. A colorful spectacle, with beautiful costumes and bright make-up, Chinese opera dates back many centuries. The operas include singing, dance, mime, and acrobatics, and use both traditional stories and up-to-date scripts. Chinese opera can be seen at theaters such as the Ko Shan Theatre in Kowloon.

Movies

Hong Kong has many movie theaters and remains one of the few places in the world where locally produced movies are consistently more popular than the latest Hollywood blockbusters. It has been a center for making movies since the 1950s and was at its height in the 1980s and 1990s. Hong Kong movies tend to be nonstop action films, and two of the most famous names associated with them are Bruce Lee and Jackie Chan.

Out and About

Hong Kong has a surprisingly large number of wild places where people can escape from the stresses and strains of city life. In the New Territories and on the islands, they can climb mountains, enjoy secluded beaches, and take forest walks. Hikers can explore several long-distance hiking trails, such as the MacLehose Trail in the New Territories or the Lantau Trail, which circles Lantau

island. An abundance of wildlife flourishes in Hong Kong, from snakes and macaques to the rare pink dolphins that inhabit the coastal waters of the South China Sea.

Sports

Hong Kong hosts some major sporting events, including the International Rugby Sevens (a rugby tournament played with seven players in each team) and the Hong

▲ *Hong Kong has many areas of great natural beauty that offer escape from the noise and pace of its urban areas.*

Kong Marathon. The most popular spectator sport in Hong Kong is horse racing, which gives residents a chance to indulge in some legal gambling. Racing takes place at the Happy Valley Racecourse on Hong Kong Island and also at Sha Tin in the New Territories. Hong Kong residents have many opportunities to participate in sports of all kinds, from sailing and windsurfing to mountain biking. Martial arts remain popular, and, in the early morning, Hong Kong's parks are full of people practising *taiji*—a form that is particularly popular with the elderly citizens.

▼ Race day at the Happy Valley Racecourse on Hong Kong Island fills the stands. Horses and the lottery are Hong Kong's only legal forms of betting.

Mahjong

The streets and alleys of residential Hong Kong often resound with a clicking sound accompanied by shouts—the sounds of mahjong players casting their tiles. Mahjong is a hugely popular game that dates back thousands of years. Players select or discard plastic tiles of different suits and values in order to form groups or sequences. Each game is a social event that can last for many hours and that usually involves much noise and happy excitement.

CHAPTER 6

Looking Forward

From the time it became a British colony, Hong Kong's greatest asset has been its hardworking and talented people. During the time of uncertainty between the announcement of the handover to China and 1997, however, many Hong Kong residents chose to emigrate abroad rather than face living under Chinese rule. This emigration peaked after the events in Tiananmen Square in Beijing in 1989, when student pro-democracy demonstrators were massacred by the tanks and guns of the Chinese People's Liberation Army. In 1992, 66,000 people emigrated from Hong Kong, primarily to Canada, Australia, and the United States.

Predictions

Many people predicted that Hong Kong would continue to prosper economically after the 1997 handover, while its democratic rights would be quietly worn away by the Chinese government. It seems, however, that the opposite may be happening. Hong Kong has had a hard time economically since 1997, owing to the downturn in the Asian market and to problems such as SARS. Meanwhile, ten years after Tiananmen Square, Hong Kong

◀ *Spectacular modern architecture characterizes the business district, but Hong Kong also offers areas of great natural beauty.*

Hong Kong is in a unique position. It is part of China yet separate from it, and this arrangement can bring benefits both for Hong Kong and for China. The future of Hong Kong depends largely on the careful balancing act between retaining its own identity and integrating with the mainland. Hong Kong is extremely important to China, both financially and commercially. In return, until 2047 at least, the people of Hong Kong will continue to enjoy democratic freedom and a more capitalistic lifestyle than people in communist China.

Tourism

The government of Hong Kong is actively promoting tourism as a major part of Hong Kong's future. Several plans to attract more tourists include building a cable car system on Lantau Island that will link Tung Chung to the Big Buddha (an enormous bronze statue of the seated Buddha) 4 miles (6.5 km) away; also, a huge "Adventure Bay" attraction at Ocean Park; and new waterfront promenades on both sides of Victoria Harbour. The biggest tourist attraction for the future, however, is likely to be the world's fourth Disneyland, at Penny Bay in the east of Lantau Island. Opening in 2005, it is expected to attract 1.5 million extra tourists to Hong Kong every year.

residents were able to freely stage a huge demonstration involving more than one million people to mark the anniversary of the massacre. Furthermore, in 2003, a controversial "anti-subversion" bill, which critics claimed would curb freedoms to criticize government, was withdrawn after huge public demonstrations in Hong Kong.

"The world is beating a path to China's door—and we have the keys to success in that massive market."

—Donald Tsang, Chief Secretary of Hong Kong, 2003.

Time Line

1839–1842 The First Opium War is fought between China and Britain.

1841 China cedes Hong Kong Island to Britain.

1856–1860 The Second Opium War between China and Britain is waged.

1860 Kowloon and Stonecutter's Island are ceded by China to Britain.

1888 The Peak Tram is opened.

1898 China leases the New Territories to Britain for ninety-nine years.

1911 Sun Yat-sen overthrows the Qing dynasty and establishes the Republic of China. The University of Hong Kong is officially founded.

1941 The Japanese occupy Hong Kong.

1945 World War II and the Japanese occupation come to an end.

1949 In China, the Communists defeat the Nationalists, and Mao Zedong declares the People's Republic of China.

1953 Fire breaks out in a squatter settlement at Shek Kip Mei, making 53,000 people homeless

1966 Riots break out in Hong Kong. In China the Cultural Revolution begins.

1976 Mao Zedong dies.

1979 The Mass Transit Railway opens in Hong Kong.

1982 The British prime minister, Margaret Thatcher, visits Hong Kong and Beijing to discuss the future of the colony.

1984 The Chinese and British joint declaration concerning the future of the colony is signed and announced.

1985 Hong Kong Academy of the Performing Arts opens.

1988 The Basic Law is published.

1989 The massacre of students and citizens in Tiananmen Square, Beijing, sparks huge demonstrations in Hong Kong.

1992 Chris Patten is appointed the last governor of Hong Kong.

1997 Hong Kong is handed back to China.

1998 Chek Lap Kok airport opens.

2002 Tung Chee-hwa is elected chief executive for a second term.

2003 The SARS epidemic hits Hong Kong, abating in 2004.

2004 The largest Hong Kong demonstration to honor Tiananmen Square protestors draws demonstrators from mainland China, who are not allowed to protest in their own country.

Glossary

Cantopop the name for Hong Kong's local style of pop music, written in Cantonese.

capitalism a political and economic system that is based on the private ownership and running of industries and businesses without government interference or control.

colony an overseas territory that has been acquired by a foreign country.

Communism a political system that strives to create a society in which everyone is equal. One of its central principles is the communal ownership of all property. Communism in China has been deeply influenced by the country's leader, Mao Zedong, from 1949 to 1976.

container ship a large cargo ship that carries its load in train-car-sized metal containers. Containers can be loaded by crane directly from one form of transportation to another.

Cultural Revolution a movement started by Mao Zedong in 1966 that attacked the four "olds": old ideas, old culture, old customs, and old habits. Chaos followed as schools and universities were closed. Many were sent to the countryside for "re-education." It ended with the death of Mao in 1976.

democracy a country ruled by popular vote, in which citizens freely elect their government in regular elections.

dynasty a period during which the rule of a country is held by a family that passes control from one generation to another.

economy a country's system of trade and industry, by which wealth is produced and distributed.

epidemic an outbreak of an infectious disease that attacks many people in one place at one time and can spread quickly.

feng shui means literally "wind and water" and is an ancient Chinese system used to work out how buildings and objects should be positioned. It is based on the principle that an invisible energy, called *qi*, flows through and around us.

Five Clans settlers in the New Territories during the Song dynasty (960–1279), the five clans are the Tang, Pang, Hai, Liu, and Man. Members of the Five Clans remain influential in the political life of Hong Kong today.

funicular a mountain railroad with two cars that balance each other and are pulled and lowered by cables wound around a drum at the top.

gross domestic product (GDP) a method of assessing the economic performance of a country or region by adding together the value of all the goods and services produced in a given period—usually a year.

handover the return of Hong Kong to China by Britain in 1997.

junk a Chinese sailing boat.

Mandarin the standard form of Chinese and the official language of the People's Republic of China.

monarch a ruler of a nation or head of state who usually has inherited the title.

Nationalist Party (also known as the Kuomintang) Founded by Sun Yat-sen in 1919, the Nationalists fought (and lost to) the Communists for control of China.

opium a substance obtained from the seeds of the opium poppy. Among other things, opium contains morphine and is addictive.

Opium Wars two wars fought in the 1800s between China and Britain over trading rights, and particularly over the illegal opium trade.

particulates tiny particles of dirt, often produced by cars, which can cause pollution.

quarantine a period of compulsory isolation to prevent the spread of disease and infection.

recession a period when a country's trade, economy, and employment is in decline.

SARS (Severe Acute Respiratory Syndrome) a pneumonia virus that originated in southern China in 2002 and reached Hong Kong in February 2003.

Special Administrative Region (SAR) The status of Hong Kong within China for fifty years, from 1997 until 2047. During this time, China will not impose its economic or political systems on the former colony.

taiji (t'ai chi) a martial art that involves shadow boxing. It is a form of *wushu* (kung fu), and dates back over 2,500 years.

typhoon the name given to hurricanes in the western north Pacific region. Wind speeds can reach up to 160 miles (260 km) per hour.

Further Information

Books

Fallon, Steve, *Lonely Planet Hong Kong & Macau: City Guide*. Lonely Planet, 2004.

Kagda, Falaq, *Cultures of the World: Hong Kong*. Benchmark Books, 1998.

Krucker, Franz-Josef, *Insight Compact Guide: Hong Kong*. Insight Guides, 2002.

Macdonald, Phil (Ed.), *National Geographic Traveler: Hong Kong*. National Geographic, 2002.

McMahon, Patricia, *Six Words, Many Turtles, and Three Days in Hong Kong*. Houghton Mifflin, 1998

Zurlo, Tony, *The Way People Live: Life in Hong Kong*. Lucent Books, 2002.

Web Sites

www.info.gov.hk
Explore the official Hong Kong government information web site.

www.lcsd.gov.hk/CE/Museum/History/english/
Learn more from the Hong Kong Museum of History.

www.legco.gov.hk/english/index.htm
Discover the "young version" of Hong Kong history.

www.marimri.com/content/hong_kong
Gather general information about Hong Kong.

www.marimari.com/content/hong_kong/best_of/chinese_opera/main.html
Pursue additonal information about Chinese opera

Index